History W

Hastings

Rye to Hastings

A Choice of Routes

This guide contains all the step by step instructions necessary to complete the walk successfully although you should always take the correct OS Maps with you in case of difficulty.

Additionally, this walk has also been added to the Ordnance Survey Walking Routes.

For a complete mapping experience, download the OS Map App, scan the QR Code and follow the route on your phone.

Information

Maps: OS Explorer 124 & 125

Route A   11.85 miles

Allow: Minimum 4+ hours

Total Ascent: 711ft

(*see notes Page 9*)

Route B   11.90 miles

Allow: Minimum 5½+ hours

Total Ascent: 1308ft

(*see notes Page 9*)

Parking

- Hastings: Pay and Display
- Fairlight: On Street
- Winchelsea: On Street
- Rye: Pay and Display

Stagecoach Buses

Route 100/101 from Hastings serves Fairlight, Winchelsea and Rye

Southern Trains   Hastings to Rye

Refreshments

- Fairlight: Coastguards Tea Room, ¼ mile
- Fairlight Cove: The Cove
- Pett Level: C-Side Cafe
- Winchelsea:
    - The New Inn,
    - The Little Shop (Takeaway Tea & Coffee)
- Rye: Many and varied

Hastings to Rye & Rye to Hastings

Whichever direction you choose to walk, either from 'Hastings to Rye' or 'Rye to Hastings' (the phrase just slips off the tongue) both are Cinque Ports and both have a long history and linked together by a road and rail and this walking guide joins public footpaths between the two towns.

The walk instructions relate first to 'Hastings to Rye' at **Page 11**, with the instructions for 'Rye to Hastings' starting at **Page 26**. The history remains the same and the maps for Rye to Hastings have been reversed to ease your progress.

A Choice of Routes

The first walk, Route A, can be taken at a more leisurely pace that enjoys, or rather avoids, the rather more extreme second route of the coastal path to Fairlight, and is a walk that can be enjoyed by people with at least a little country walking experience.

The second walk, Route B, is a little bit more of a challenge, at least for the walk to or from Fairlight. This 'undulating' coastal route is just as demanding as parts of the Cornish Coastal Path and is enough to set the pulse racing with steps, steepish descents and over 1000 feet to climb.

Note: If the weather is bad or conditions very wet, Route B can be very heavy going, with some of the uphills and downhills treacherous to walk – better to wait for harder ground or choose Route A.

The reward for all the effort is a quick jog down to The Cove at Fairlight Cove for a well-deserved pint and with the bus stop just outside take you to Hastings or Rye, you can choose to finish the walk another day.

This walk can be completed in one go and you can catch the bus or train back from either Rye or Hastings.

Walk what you are happy with, after all 12 miles is still 12 miles whether you walk it all in one go or over a couple of days. Even the climb up to East Hill can be circumvented for, if the steps are too daunting, you can always ride up on the East Hill Lift, the steepest funicular railway in the UK.

Both walks are split into the same three sections: Hastings to Fairlight, Fairlight to Winchlesea Bridge and Winchelsea Bridge to Rye, and the same in reverse, handy for a Stagecoach bus back to Hastings and Rye. There is a pub at the end to celebrate each walk and the chance to explore Hastings, Winchelsea, Camber Castle and Rye.

Either route **can** be walked in a day, with time to spare, although I did leave the rest and recuperation until the end. Take sandwiches for a picnic halfway (on the beach at Pett Level) but if you are travelling light the C-Side Cafe by the sea wall does food (see Page 37).

Reflections

You are about to walk one of the most picturesque and historic routes in the South-East of England and it is surprising that is not walked more often.

Hastings Old Town is still a delightful mix of half-timbered houses, narrow streets and passageways, and home to the largest beach-launched fishing fleet in Europe. However, the Old Town will need to be explored on another day as this walk climbs up to East Hill. Winchelsea and Rye are similarly historic and both need a little time to discover their unique charms and sample the hospitality.

This walk will reflect the changing coastline and the threat of war and invasion. It is a stretch of sea that has long been England's defence against invasion but this ever-changing coastline has battles of its own to fight. The Sussex coast has always suffered from violent storms and with the additional hazard of longshore drift, the eastward movement of shingle along the coast, the coastline has frequently changed.

1000 years ago, the sea held sway over the great marshes and lapped far up the valleys and coves, creating safe havens for the local boats but also providing the opportunity for Danish and Viking marauders to enjoy a little local looting, pillage and whatever else caught their eye. Hastings was one such haven, the sea stretching far up the valley of what is now Priory Meadow, below the West Hill. It was only after the Norman invasion that Hastings began to grow along the Bourne Valley, now Old Town. Before that, there was a Hastings settlement and a port when the Romans arrived in Britain, in 55 BC, but the first mention of Hastingas would have to wait for King Offa of Mercia to win a battle over the *Hestingorum gens (the people of the Hastings tribe),* in 771AD.

In 1066, Hastings became synonymous with Duke William of Normandy, although the famous battle that decided the future of England was fought seven miles north along the Senlac Ridge. Hastings became Duke William's base, where he built a temporary wooden castle on West Hill.

Hastings had been carefully chosen as it was under the control of the Norman Bishop of Fécamp, through ownership of the Saxon Manor of 'Rameslie' that was gifted to the Abbey by King Canute. This Fécamp connection proved valuable for Hastings, Winchelsea and Rye as it gave some protection from the rampaging Norman knights as they sought to gain control over Wessex whereas, Saxon Bexhill to the west and Romney to the east were amongst villages sacked and burnt.

Cinque Ports

The Cinque Ports provided ships for cross-Channel trade, communication and acted as a part time navy and the ports of Winchelsea and Rye were linked closely to Hastings. Coastal erosion, sea damage and silting reduced the effectiveness of Hastings as a port. The ports of Rye and Winchelsea quickly outgrew Hastings until, the great storms of the late 13th century, when serious flooding damaged most of Hastings along the Bourne and swept away old Winchelsea.

The new coastline allowed the creation of Pett Level and Romney Marsh, changed the course of the River Rother and drained the great Appledore Estuary behind Rye.

There was major damage to the cliffs from Hastings to Pett Level and much of Hasting Castle slipped into the sea. In the 18th century, the West Hill cliff was further cut back to allow the building of a road, from the Old Town to the New Town, and the development of Pelham Crescent that can be seen at the start of the walk. Once the move away from the old town had begun, it led to further expansion along the coast, eventually linking up with the new Burton St Leonards.

But Hastings, Winchelsea and especially Rye never lost their link to the sea for the wide expanse and easy beach at Pett Level, and the many coves and inlets that line the cliffs from Hastings to Pett Level, saw the growth of another industry, smuggling and there was money to be made.

Smuggling

By the 18th century, an agricultural depression lay over Sussex and Kent and when George III prohibited the export of wool and cloth, which was much in demand in France and Flanders, the mill owners and farmers saw the opportunity for profit. Wool was smuggled out of England and when the boats returned they were loaded with wines, spirits, tea and silk. Large scale importing of contraband initially came about as a means of paying for the wool.

The situation was endemic involving a great proportion of the local population in Kent and Sussex, whatever their level in society. Certain people became very rich on the proceeds but a large portion of the population also benefitted and it was rarely seen as a crime except by the government, the magistrates and the Revenue men.

The most notorious smuggling coasts of Britain during the eighteenth century, were in East Kent and in particular those bordering on Romney Marsh. Some reasons for this are obvious; the Kent shores lay nearest to continental suppliers and many of the beaches were ideal for undisturbed landings. Ecclesbourne Glen, Fairlight Glen, Warren Glen, Fairlight Cove and Pett Level were similarly remote and the tracks and paths inland led directly to Burwash and Hawkhurst.

Although Coast Blockade Service Watch Houses were built at Ecclesbourne Glen, The Haddocks and Pett Level early in the 1800's, smuggling would continue well into the 19th century and it is still easy to imagine boats being landed and their cargo carried up the paths away from the beaches.

Rye

This 'ancient town' was once an important port at the head of the great Appledore Estuary but the great storms of the 13th and 14th centuries changed the coastline forever and marooned the town more than two miles inland. Now it stands guarding the marshes with its fishing fleet confined to the River Rother.

Rye too was under the control of the Abbey of Fécamp, Norman in all but name, which gave it some protection. Two hundred years later, amidst the turmoil of the 100 Years War with the French, the town was regularly raided and finally in 1377 the French burnt almost everything to the ground and pinched the bells of St Mary's Church. Afterwards, and a little too late, the town began to be fortified and enclosed the narrow, cobbled streets and atmospheric houses which have left Rye with its unique identity.

Unsurprisingly, Rye drew the notorious Hawkhurst gang into its inns and pubs and the stories of murder and mayhem are legion, retold by Mary Waugh in her 'Smuggling in Kent and Sussex 1700 to 1840'. Nowadays, it is safer to wander the streets and follow the many town guides that explore the history of Rye in greater detail than space in this booklet allows – after all this is a walking book.

* Route A

The High Route' (Route A) is less demanding and allows those not used to steepish climbs and descents to still have the satisfaction of walking between Hastings and Rye on what has been called one of the best walking routes in England. Route A is considered to be a 'Leisure Walk' for reasonably fit people with at least a little country walking experience along public footpaths and tracks and walking shoes or boots are recommended.

Between Pett Level and Rye, the walk is flatter over the marshes by the Royal Military Canal.

Remember that you may need warm, waterproof clothing depending on the time of year and the conditions.

If you intend taking your dog on this walk, remember that, for much of the walk through Hastings Country Park, your dog is only a fence away from eternity or doggy paradise and that lead may be essential rather than an accessory. After Pett Level, the marshes are home to sheep and again it is recommended that dogs be kept on the lead.

** Route B

The first, or last section follows 'The Saxon Shore Way' (Route B) and is strenuous and can be a challenge although it is rewarding when completed. It is of 'Moderate Plus' difficulty and is a walk for people with country walking experience and a good level of fitness. It includes some steep paths and open country where walking boots are preferred, depending on conditions.

Decisions, Decisions – Route A or Route B?

These path profiles will help you decide the route for you.

For route A, the hard part is climbing the steps up to East Hill, after that the gradients are far gentler to and from Rye.

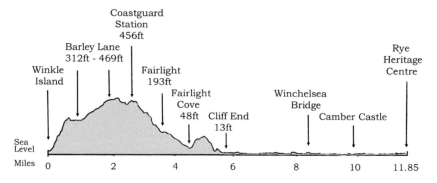

Route B is up and down with around 450 metres to climb - a good walk in the knowledge that it will get easier and the views are worth the challenge.

From Hastings, you are safe in the knowledge that it will get easier.

From Rye, the hard part are those final five miles but as a challenge, it is worth it.

A. Ecclesbourne Glen
B. Warren   Glen
C. Fairlight Glen

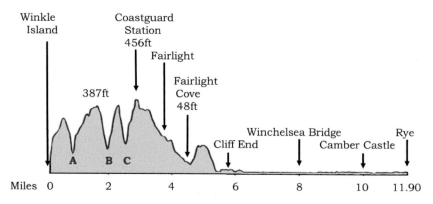

You choose!

Hastings to Rye

Hastings to East Hill

Distance: 0.50 miles Allow: 25 minutes

The start is at the iconic Winkle Island with its story board about the famous Hastings Winkle Club (next to the shiny winkle) Winkle Island.

Across the road is The Hastings Contemporary opened in 2012 and styled in a similar dark wood vein to the black and almost gothic net shops that line the road. It features contemporary art in both permanent and temporary collections. Together they are more than a fitting start to the walk to Rye.

Walk along Rock-a-Nore Road towards The Dolphin, past the first of Hasting's unique Net Huts, and climb the Tamarisk Steps on the left-hand side of the pub, the start of the 218 steps up to East Hill.

Turn right halfway up, signposted East Hill, and at the top of the steps turn left along Tackleway and then, almost immediately, turn right to complete the climb up towards the head of the funicular railway and the beginning of Hastings Country Park *(the park came into being 1st April 1971, three quarters of which is officially designated as being of Special Scientific Interest).*

The steps are not too bad once you start and you climb high very quickly with views looking back to the fishing fleet, Marine Court and in the distance, Beachey Head. *Of course, if the steps up to the East Hill are too daunting you can always ride up in style on the East Hill Lift, I won't tell if you don't tell!*

At the top of the steps, bear right up just a few more steps to follow the waymarks for The Saxon Shore Way, keeping to the sea side of East Hill and heading up towards the top of the hill. The beacon stands proud and is traditionally lit for special occasions and on the night of Hastings Bonfire.

On a fine day, the ships on the horizon seem to glide effortlessly by, the white sails of the yachts play and maybe the boats of the Hastings fishing fleet can be seen. But, imagine it is a rainy overcast day with the wind whipping up the white horses, the Dover ferry has stayed in port, the horizon has all but disappeared and yes that is the light of a Hastings fishing boat, determinedly battling the elements for that all important catch of the day.

At the summit of East Hill, it is decision time, the final chance to decide Route A or Route B (Page 14)?

The Hard Route, Route B, follows 'The Saxon Shore Way' and all the ups and downs of the coastal path and known to my daughter Hannah and me as 'The Four Peaks Challenge'. Route B re-joins Route A on the approach to Fairlight, below the Coastguard Station, for a gentle stroll into the village.

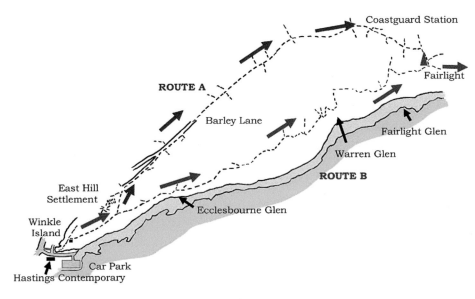

Route A

East Hill to the Coastguard Station Distance 2.35 miles Allow: 1 hr

The walk follows first the '1066 Country Walk' and then the public footpath to the Coastguard Station. It is a gently rising and descending route that avoids the strenuous ups and downs of the coastal path.

Bear left to walk to the right of the site of the Iron Age Settlement and the BBQ area, towards the exit from the country park into Rocklands Lane, the waymarks point down a track that levels out and joins the metalled road to Barley Lane.

On this grey November day, the hedges sheltered me from the blustery winds over East Hill and it began to feel warm.

Continue along Rocklands Lane towards Barley Lane, bear right at the junction and walk to the end of Barley Lane.

It is a gentle climb of half a mile, ignoring any footpaths off either side, and at the T junction, you will have climbed to 469ft from sea level, high but not quite the highest point of this section.

There is a 'Sustrans' post, National Cycle Network, that shows two miles from Hastings in 40 minutes but Dover is 50 miles away, perhaps another day!

Cross the road through the kissing gate and along the well-trod path straight ahead.

Here there is mud, there is almost always mud and the pace drops a little. In front and slightly to the right are the line of Coastguard Cottages that signals that Fairlight village is not too far away.

In a gap in the trees is a view of the sea but there will be better views closer to the Coastguard Station.

This section after Barley Lane to the Coastguard Cottages undulates up and down, a high point of 489ft is passed unnoticed as more mud is negotiated, it is November after all and I can look forward to drier paths during spring and summer.

Through the kissing gate and walk down and then up to exit through two more kissing gates onto the track. Cross over and follow the clear waymarked path ahead.

Waymarks confirm Firehills and then Fairlight 1½ miles and the path opens out to views over the Channel and the wind picks up once again.

A large container ship sails by, hardly distinguishable today, grey on grey sea and grey sky, the radar dish on the headland sweeps round and monitors the ship's every nautical mile.

A final short climb up to the marker post in front. Bear right through a gate to follow the tarmac path towards the Coastguard Cottages in front. At the end, turn right and walk down the lane past this windswept terrace.

On a clear day, there is the broad sweep of the marshes and Rye Bay to savour but today, it all merges into a grey mist although, with the wind at my back and no rain, it has been good walking weather.

At the bottom of the lane by the coastguard station bear right through the gate and walk down to meet the path from Warren Glen and turn left to continue along the coastal path to Fairlight.

It is downhill now to Fairlight and Fairlight Cove as Route A and Route B combine for the rest of the walk to Rye. (Page 17)

Route B:

East Hill to the Coastguard Station Distance 2.40 miles Allow: 1½ hrs

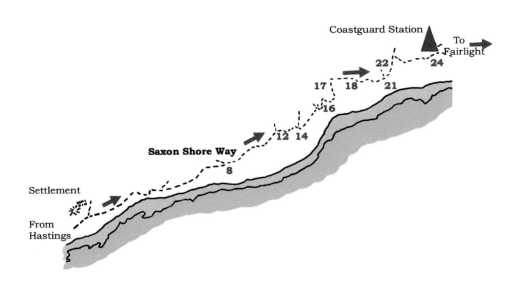

At the summit of East Hill, close to the site of the Iron Age settlement, keep right and follow the path down the hill towards the steps, through the trees and down to Ecclesbourne Glen.

Walk across the little bridge and up steps that appear to have been built for giants.

This heavily wooded valley was once the landing place and entrance for the Iron Age Hill Fort at the centre of East Hill.

At the top, turn right towards the bench and the viewing point that overlooks the harbour, Rock-a-Nore and Ecclesbourne Glen.

(In 1890, a Harbour Act was passed and construction began on Hastings Harbour to include two long harbour arms and a railway through a tunnel to be cut in East Cliff. However, work stalled when serious difficulties were encountered by the irregular nature of the seabed and difficulties in raising more capital, leaving the unique harbour arm).

Once you've caught your breath, turn around and continue along the clear coast path towards Waypost 8. It is a broad open grass path that gives a sense of being on top of the world with the opportunity to look back at the broad sweep of Pevensey Bay that reaches all the way round to Beachey Head.

Continue along the Saxon Shore Way to Waypost 8 and bear right up the hill towards Fairlight Glen.

After the up, the down soon comes along.

Take either fork, then bear right at Post 12 to follow the sign to Fairlight Glen Lower. Down the steps, past Waypost 14 points on to Fairlight Glen.

The path weaves between trees that arch over providing shade in summer, and the sea can be glimpsed then heard as the waves crash upon the rocks below. Opposite, is the next hill to climb and the Coastguard Station can just be seen at the top but it is an illusion, as hidden from view is Warren Glen, the final down and up before the Coastguard Station is reached.

Bear right at Post 16 (towards Warren Glen) and the bottom of Fairlight Glen is soon reached to start the longest uphill climb of the section.

The path starts to meander up more steps to a handy bench before heading inland up and away from the sea and the climb becomes more gradual.

It is a moment to stop and imagine a time two hundred years ago on a dark night either here or at Warren Glen just over the headland. 'A score of men, some standing in groups, some resting on the ground, and the dark shapes of pack horses showing larger in the dimness. There were a few muttered words of greeting as we all waited, waited for the first boat's nose to grind on the shingle. Then all fell to the business of landing and later, to file away from the beach along the paths when I saw something move behind the brambles.....'(with acknowledgement to 'Moonfleet' by J Meade Falkner)

At post 17, turn sharp right to Warren Glen (½ mile) and up the final few steps before the descent into the valley, along steps that curve down to the right.

At Post 18, continue through an annoying kissing gate, where I had to take my rucksack off to get through, and at Post 21 continue straight ahead to Firehills with just one more hill to climb. More steps and at the top turn right, Post 22 to follow the clear path up to the Coastguard Station.

Through the kissing gate at Waypost 24 to re-join Route A on the way down to Fairlight Cove, Pett Level and Rye.

In the shadow of the radar mast, Route A and Route B combine for the walk to Rye.

But stand here for a minute, at this the highest land between Beachy Head in the west and Hythe in the east and imagine the threat of invasion.

Probably from the early 13th century, watches have been kept to secure England against an attack across the channel with a network of fire beacons along the coast that would signal the presence of enemy ships.

Too late for the Norman Invasion of 1066 but in the 100 Years War, French ships would maraud across La Manche, looting and setting fire to English towns and villages. You could have watched in amazement as the Spanish Armada sailed past in 1588, and almost endless 130 ships. You could have had a birds-eye view of the Battle of Dungeness sea battle of 1652 and the immense anticipation of a French Invasion during the Napoleonic Wars and finally, the part it would play in the Second World War.

A signal station was built in 1794/5 that was upgraded over the years to monitor shipping movements, identify enemy vessels and communicate with defence forces by day and night. By 1932 it was the only constant-watch Coastguard station between Newhaven and Dungeness but later, in

1982, was downgraded, to become a secondary station, to be manned during bad weather and searches. Now the radar monitors Channel shipping.

Coastguard Station to Fairlight Cove: Distance 1 mile   Allow 20mins

From the shadow of the radar station, bear right along the grass path that sweeps down to the right, along the cliff top all the way to Channel Way. Through the kissing gate and follow the lane to take second left along Shepherd's Way.

To continue the walk to Cliff End, Pett Level and Winchelsea take the first right along Bramble Way.

For the bus to both Hastings and Rye, the stop is at the island ahead, at the junction with Commanders Walk and the pub just 5 minutes more walk away.

Fairlight Cove to Pett Level Distance 2.00 miles Allow 40 mins

If starting this section at Fairlight Cove, and having caught the Stagecoach 101 from Hastings, ask for Commanders Walk which is the nearest stop to Bramble Way.

The 101 bus ride from Hastings to Fairlight is worth the trip in itself, even if you are not walking. On a clear day, the views are superb and rival any scenic tour. The same bus continues on to Pett Level, Winchelsea Bridge and Rye and returns the same route back to Hastings.

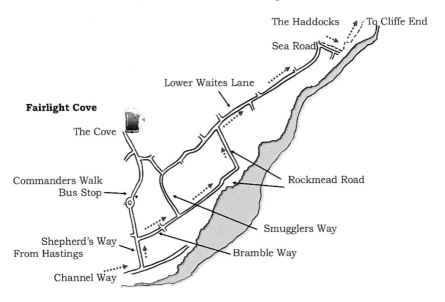

Continuing the walk from the Coastguard Station, turn left into Sheppard's Way, turn first right into Bramble Way *(or first left from the Commanders Walk bus stop)* and continue straight ahead into Rockmead Road, provided there are no warning signs of road closure.

This gravel lane runs close to the cliff edge, very close in places, and the dire warnings leave little for the imagination. Rockmead Road curves down to the left to meet Lower Waites Lane, turn right.

Lower Waites Lane starts to dip downhill to its junction with Sea Road where the footpath continues across the road, up a couple of steps and through the trees into what is named on a large-scale map as 'The Haddocks', Follow the waymark right, around the edge of the field, towards the sea.

At The Haddocks, a Coast Blockade Service (CBS) watch house was built to house a section of armed Navy men (nicknamed the Warriors) to counter the increasingly desperate smugglers using the Cove to land their brandy. The CBS was set up in 1817 to replace the 1809-formed Preventive Water Guard and after 1832, when smuggling declined, they took on a more life-saving role as Coastguards.

Continue along the path, first left and then right and left again, and suddenly the sound of the waves crashing against the rocks is very close and you realise how near you are to the cliff edge.

The path begins to climb towards the bench ahead and an ideal spot to stop and look back at Fairlight.

The coastguard cottages are set low on the horizon above the village and below are the cliffs at Fairlight, with houses perilously close to a cliff edge that has been damaged both by high sea and rains leading to land slips. Sea defences have been put in place and there are plans for new defences that are forecast to save 161 properties over the next 100 years but it is likely that some will still disappear into the sea.

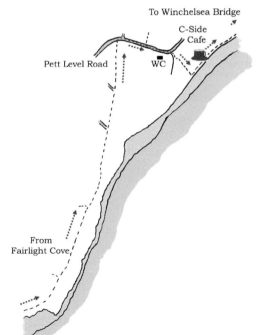

Up the steps to the left of the bench and continue the path eastwards, parallel to the cliff edge and as the path curves gradually around to the left, a white chimney stack can just be seen above the trees. Roof tops come into view and the footpath starts to descend past a marker post for The National Trust 'Fairlight', that owns this section of the coastline

It would seem that all that separates the houses on the left from the sea on the right is the width of this path. Delightful setting it may be but they must want or like living with the danger.

The waymark bears left and continue downhill straight ahead.

I would not want to go right! - and down below is the whole stretch of the beach and a coastline that curves all the way round to Dungeness. Closer, down by the beach below, is the path on top of the sea wall that passes the

C-Side café and The New Beach Club (Members Only) and connects to the Royal Military Canal and the path to Winchelsea.

Although reasonably dry today I would imagine, from the gully that has been eroded in the middle of the path, that in heavy rain this footpath downhill is likely to be a bit of a torrent.

At the bottom, turn right towards the sea but take care, there is no footpath.

By the small car park, and the toilet block on the right, is a story board that provides some of the history of the Royal Military Canal.

Ignore the footpath waymark on the other side of the road and walk towards the bend where the public footpath towards the beach is to the left of the substantial stone gate posts in front.

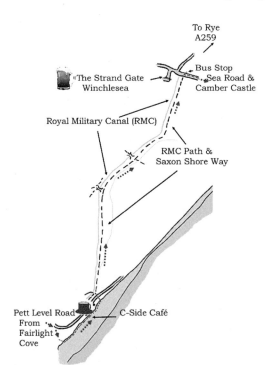

Walk up the drive and follow the waymark left, up a couple of steps, across the sand to climb up to the sea wall and turn left, past the caravan site nestling down out of the wind.

On this grey breezy day, there is an artist sat on the shingle, a tent for shelter, looking back towards the cliffs which are impressive and no doubt a must for fossil collectors.

The C-Side café is on the left by the 'The Pett Level Independent Rescue Centre and Look Out Post'.

On the small ridge behind the houses stands Toot Rock and silhouetted against the sky, is the WW2 Battery Observation Post that commanded a two-gun battery and controlled a purposefully flooded Pett Level that was part of the coastal defence in case of invasion.

Pett Level to Winchelsea Bridge Distance: 3.00 Allow: 1 hour

Continue along the path along the sea wall.

Here the designer styled houses poke their upper floors above the parapet for views of the sea, including one featured on 'Grand Designs' painted white and imaginatively called - 'The White House'.

Past the New Beach Club.

And past the first ramp that descends on the left, past the first set of steps and head towards and down the second set of steps where Pett Level Road begins to curve right.

From the top of the sea wall, the Royal Military Canal (RMC) stretches away towards Winchelsea across the serenity of the marsh. 800 years ago, all this flat land was under water until the coastline was irrevocably changed by the great storms of the 13th century and so far, the sea has not yet reclaimed its birthright.

Cross the road and follow the waymark, past a white rock called 'Toot Rock', down the concrete lane that once led to the Toot Rock Coastguard Station. At the finger post, turn right to follow the waymarked path along the south bank of the canal.

The RMC was a massive undertaking, designed as a defence against Napoleon, but was not fully finished until 1809 some four years after the Battle of Trafalgar and the threat of invasion had passed. The canal runs for 28 miles from Cliff End to Seabrook, near Folkestone and was designed to be 19 metres wide at the surface, 13.5 metres wide at the bottom and 3 metres deep. The excavated soil was piled on to the north bank to make a defensive parapet where the army could be positioned out of sight of the French. The canal is 'kinked' with bends right and left at regular intervals and allowed a greater field of fire along the length of the canal, a clever concept that can still be seen. Today, the RMC helps with the drainage of the marsh which is perhaps more relevant.

On this Monday morning, the breeze just ruffles the grass as the sun tries to make an impression but the solitude is disturbed not by the sea but by the cars on the road. Plaintiff bird calls emphasise wildness but the cattle on the north bank, all lying down in readiness for tomorrow's forecast rain, appear unmoved and watch nonchalantly as I pass.

There has been little rain over the last few days but the path by the canal is still muddy and there is standing water in the fields, the water table must be high.

Six inquisitive dogs, all different sizes, all on leads, and all wanting a pat on the head, fuss by with their two 'carers'.

For some reason the canal is dry today, just a trickle in the bottom, whereas the dyke on the right is reasonably full. Further research would suggest that it is part of the grand design for flood relief allowing space for run off from the anticipated winter rains. In summer, its level is likely to be much higher.

The canal bears left and the track with a better covering of grass is easier to walk on with the damp grass cleaning my boots.

A squat way post tells me that I have walked one mile from Pett Level and that there is still five miles to walk to Rye, give or take a ½ mile.

On the horizon to the left is a sail-less windmill on Hog Hill that is still Sir Paul McCartney's recording studio.

Ignore the bridge and the footpath off to the left and continue straight ahead to the gate with the stile to the right but just be careful, especially when it is wet, one slip and you could end up in the dyke, a soggy end to a good walk.

Past the second bridge and continue along the south bank of the canal for another mile.

It has been a long section along the RMC, a relentless, perhaps tedious walk along the flat canal bank where it is so easy to pick up the pace. There is a beauty about the marsh, even on this November day, and Pett Level deserves a little more of our time to appreciate the landscape and the isolation. A car crosses the bridge in front and to the left, up in the ridge, hidden by the trees, is the first sign of Winchelsea itself. Seaward is a long spreading ribbon of houses and caravans that mark Winchelsea Beach.

Suddenly the air is rent by the sound of rooks, their harsh voices echo against the trees, disturbed from their nests by some hidden travesty, circling and swooping without order until the command is given that it is safe to return to their nests and peace is restored.

There is still ten minutes to walk to 'that' bridge and up above is one of Winchelsea's Gates, the Strand or Watchbell Gate. It stands guard over the south of the town still looking out for attack from the south with the remnants of the Town Wall to the east of the gate.

If you want or need to visit Winchelsea, turn left at Sea Road onto the A259 and then turn left up Strand Hill to walk between the arch of the Strand Gate.

It is a generous two hours from Fairlight and I am ready now for a change in perspective on the way to Rye. Although it is never that far away, I leave the canal behind for a mile or two before it joins up with the River Brede that flows towards Rye. I stopped for a drink by a stile and stopped again for a chat with two couples from Beckley, out for a circular walk from Winchelsea.

Winchelsea Bridge to Rye   Distance 3.00 miles Allow 1 hour

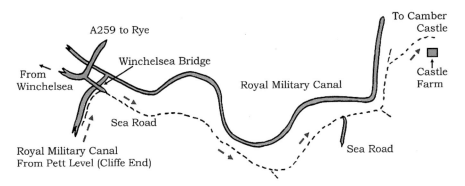

For Rye, turn right at Sea Road *(the bus stop back to Fairlight and Hastings is just across the road)* and walk for just over ½ a mile past bungalows, houses and chalets, permanent homes and holiday cottages, B&Bs and 'Sutton's Deli' with all kinds of game and fish for sale.

Sea Road bends right and then left and as the road makes an acute turn right continue straight ahead following the waymarks for The Saxon Shore Way and the Royal Military Canal Path.

The lane curves round to the left, then, take the right-hand fork towards and past Castle Farm and waymarks confirm the direction.

To the left are the first views of Camber Castle marooned in the marsh, squat and sturdy, small but beautifully formed and at the time, the cutting edge in castle design. Behind the castle, sitting proudly and keeping a watch over the marsh is Rye.

Keep following the meandering lane that has become little more than a track. Bear left to follow the waymarks and then, after less than 50

metres, bear left through the gate to follow the left-hand track that curves round towards the Castle and leads to a gate with waymarks that point to Rye.

Having walked from Hastings, and although Rye is so close, it would have been churlish not to explore the castle.

Camber Castle was built on a shingle spit between 1539 and 1544 to provide artillery protection for shipping entering Rye and Winchelsea and for a short time it was important defensively but the changing shoreline soon left it high and dry. Ideally, I would have liked a bench to sit and drink my tea and contemplate a time 500 years ago when Camber was in its glory, but there was no bench anywhere around the castle, more's the pity, so without a seat and 'tealess' and with the Castle closed for the winter (open 1st June to 30th September) I walked around the walls to re-join the main path to the finish.

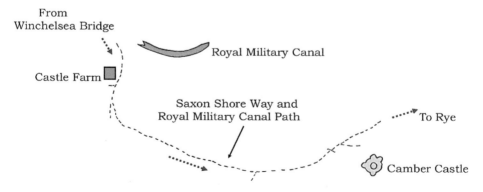

From the gate, follow the waymarks, with the barbed wire fence to the left, towards the well-preserved World War Two concrete air raid shelter.

Through the gate on the left, over the dyke and follow the waymark to the right, heading towards the row of houses that line the River Brede. Bear right again to continue along the track by the dyke and up ahead are the masts of the boats in the boatyard that lines the river.

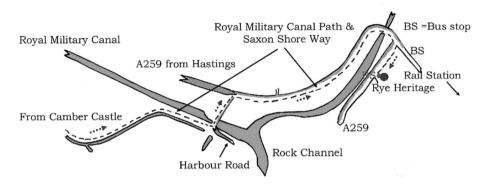

Through the gate and into the drive that leads to Harbour Road and turn left. Over the footbridge and at the A259, New Winchelsea Road, turn right for the final ½ mile to the finish at Rye Heritage Centre that can be seen on the eastern bank of the River Brede close to what were the net shops.

In front is a windmill and at the roundabout, turn right for the Heritage Centre which is a few metres down on the left.

The closest bus stop is just along Wish Street which is straight ahead at the island instead of turning right.

At the island, you have a choice to either celebrate with fish and chips from the Kettle o' Fish or tea and cake at the café. For anything stronger there are pubs galore further into town, the closest of which is The Ship, behind the net shops.

But climb Mermaid Hill and visit the Mermaid and you enter the realms of one of the most notorious smuggler's pub of the 18th century for The Mermaid was the home from home for the Hawkhurst Gang.

Today, when you enter The Mermaid, you should look very carefully for hidden away in a corner might be sitting that most famous pirate of all - 'Captain Horatio Pugwash, Captain of the Black Pig' – but only for those of a certain age! *(John Ryan, the creator of the comic strip lived in Rye).*

Rye to Hastings

Route A   11.85 miles

Allow: Minimum 4+ hours

Total Ascent: 711ft

(*see notes Page 9*)

Route B   11.90 miles

Allow: Minimum 5½+ hours

Total Ascent: 1308ft

(*see notes Page 9*)

Rye to Winchelsea Bridge   Distance: 3miles   Allow 1 hour

The start is at the Rye Heritage Centre on the A259, South Undercliffe.

With your back to the Centre, and facing the River Tillingham, turn right and walk towards the mini roundabout and cross the road at the zebra crossing. Continue right, over the bridge and walk along the A259, New Winchelsea Road, to Harbour Road and turn left (it is better to cross the road at the junction).

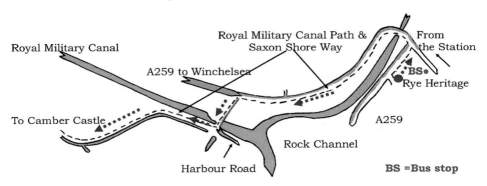

Walk towards and across the bridge over the Royal Military Canal and turn right to follow the waymarked bridleway to Winchelsea Beach.

On this section, there is likely to be a multitude of sheep grazing the marsh and it is advisable to keep dogs under close control.

Through the gates and follow the waymarks, for one mile, along the top of the flood bank towards the squat and silhouetted Camber Castle.

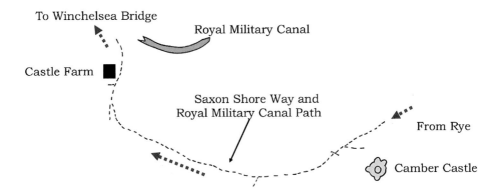

The landscape of the Rye Harbour Nature Reserve and the big sky makes an excellent start to any walk except of course when the wind and the rain are blowing into your face – today, the sun shines.

Continue along the flood bank and the bridleway and ignore the first footpath on the left. At the next marker post, bear left leaving the bridleway, through the gate and walk along the path by the fence on the right towards Camber Castle.

If your plans for the day allow, Camber Castle is worth a visit but it is better to check on the English Heritage website before you walk as opening hours are restricted.

Camber Castle is off to the left of the path – through the gate and follow the waymark, bearing slightly right – the broad green grassy path just cuts off a corner of the main track.

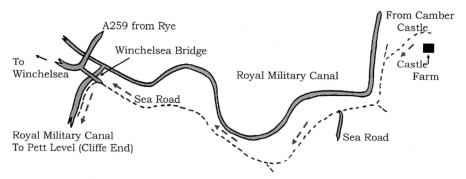

Re-join the main track and head towards the houses in front before following the path round to the right, towards Castle Farm, through the gate and continue along the lane as it wanders to Sea Road.

At the junction with Sea Road, turn right to walk the half mile to the junction with the A259. To the right are good views of the Castle and Rye and in front, Winchelsea.

Opposite the bus stop is the entrance to the Royal Military Canal Path and the route to The Smuggler. It has taken around one hour to walk from Rye and will take a similar time to The Smuggler.

However, if you want to visit historic Winchelsea and catch the bus back to Rye, continue to the A259 and walk towards and up Strand Hill on the left to walk between the arch of the Strand Gate. There is a deli and coffee shop, the parish church and graveyard and the New Inn to provide a pint before the bus ride back to Rye.

Winchelsea Bridge to Coastguard Station

Distance: 6 miles   Allow 2½ hours

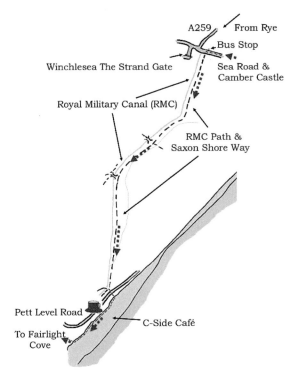

A259   From Rye

Bus Stop

Winchlesea The Strand Gate

Sea Road &
Camber Castle

Royal Military Canal (RMC)

RMC Path &
Saxon Shore Way

Pett Level Road

C-Side Café

To Fairlight
Cove

Through the kissing gate to start the walk to Pett Level, at which point there is also the option of the bus back to Rye or to continue on to Fairlight and Hastings.

This flat walk beside the Royal Military Canal, full after the winter rains, is one of solitude against the backdrop of the marsh and a feeling of isolation the further along you walk.

Ahead is Pett Level and the start of the climb up to Hastings Country Park and the Coastguard Station.

The squat tower on the horizon is Fairlight Church and the radio masts to the right are close to North's Seat.

Finally, at the concrete road, turn left to, and across, Pett Level Road, climb the steps in front and turn right to walk along the sea wall past The New Beach Club.

The C-Side café is on the right by the 'The Pett Level Independent Rescue Centre and Look Out Post' and behind the café on the road are the bus stops for Hastings and Rye.

Walk along the sea wall to the end of the Pett Level Caravan Park where there are steps on the right that lead over the wall to a drive.

There are no stiles between Pett Level and Hastings which benefits those using walking poles

Turn right and walk down to Pett Level Road and turn left to walk past the toilet block, and the small car park, and continue along Pett Level

Road for around 200 metres. Take care as there is no footpath on this short section of road.

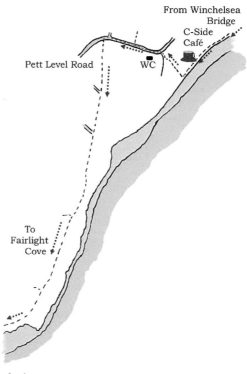

From Winchelsea Bridge

C-Side Café

Pett Level Road

WC

To Fairlight Cove

Just after the junction with Marsham Brook Lane and Chick Hill (to Pett Village) look for the drive on the left-hand side of the road that leads to the public footpath, just a few metres up on the right.

Follow the footpath, waymarked The Saxon Shore Way and Maritime Heritage Trail, up to the top of the cliffs.

The further up you walk, the closer the path runs to the cliff edge but sea defences are now in place to prevent further erosion and the houses are safe for the time being.

The National Trust Fairlight sign confirms that the cliffs are part of our heritage as the path continues parallel to the sea towards Fairlight.

Fairlight village appears as the path starts to descend to The Haddocks and Fairlight Cove.

Down the steps and follow the path right towards The Haddocks. Follow the path around the hedge and at the end, turn sharp right and continue to walk down to the bottom of the field ignoring the first exit on the left.

At the bottom corner, turn left through the opening onto Lower Waites Lane and bear left to walk up Lower Waites Lane for a ½ mile.

At the end, the lane turns left into Smuggler's Way. Walk up Smuggler's Way to the junction with Bramble Way and turn right and walk to the end of the road.

At the junction with Shepherd's Way, turn left to continue the walk to Hastings.

The bus stop, for the services to Hastings and to Rye, is to the right. Walk down to the island for the Commander's Way stop but just check as you are boarding where the bus is heading as both routes use the same stop and you would not want to end up in Hastings when you really wanted Rye or vice versa.

If you would like more of a stop, either before the bus or to recoup strength before the walk to Hastings, there is always the opportunity for a pint at The Cove, just a further few minutes along Commander's Way away from the coast.

If you choose to finish the walk another day, there are bus stop just outside The Cove to take you to Hastings or Rye.

Walk up to the junction with Channel Way and turn right and continue, on a gentle climb, to the end of the track and bear left onto the fenced in footpath to enter Hastings Country Park.

Though the kissing gate and at Post 27, take the lower path straight ahead on the left to begin the steady climb up the hill towards the Coastguard Station. where the route splits into the East Route A or the Harder Route B.

The fence on the left provides some safety from the cliff edge, except for inquisitive dogs.

This short climb helps the lungs prepare for Rout B and the adventures ahead and the top affords views along the cliffs and in the distance the Harbour wall at Hastings can just be seen.

The walk from Pett Level has taken around 1¼ hours with about 1½ hours remaining.

Route A - The Less Demanding Route

Coastguard Station to Rock a Nore Distance 2.85 miles Allow: 1 hr

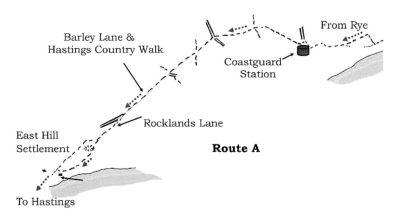

Walk up to the Coastguard Cottages, through the gate and onto the track to walk away from the sea. At the end of the cottages, turn left along the path signed 'Hastings Country Park Access for all Trails' and the first sign of Hastings comes into view and on this March day, the sea is truly aquamarine.

At the end of the hard path follow the signpost to Warren Glen and Fairlight Glen through the kissing gate and at Post 23 bear left to Warren Glen Upper and Barley Lane along the gently undulating path.

Keep heading west and Post 20 confirms the path to Barley Lane.

Immediately after Little Warren Cottage bear left along the waymarked path through the kissing gate and across the field with the fence on the left. March and the bunnies are playfully getting ready for Easter enjoying the sunshine.

Through the kissing gate and at Post 19 continue straight ahead for Barley Lane. This final section, before the road, has always been muddy, even in summer and saps the legs a little but there is always the knowledge that at Barley Lane it is all downhill to Hastings.

Through the final kissing gate, cross the road and walk down Barley Lane for one mile, following the route of the 1066 Country Walk Hastings Link, past the caravan park to the junction with Rocklands Lane where the path re-joins the more demanding walk on East Hill for the walk to Winkle Island and Hastings.

Follow the way marks for the Fish Trail and head south-west towards the post in front on top of the hill marked as a 'settlement on the OS Explorer map. At the post bear slightly right by the side of the BBQ area and walk down hill to the East Hill Lift Station and the steps

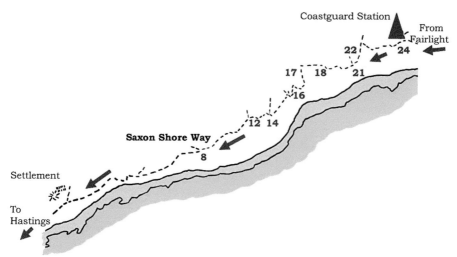

down to Rock-a-Nore – it is easier to use that great concrete liner, Marine Court marooned on the seafront, as heading.

Route B Challenging but Scenic

Coastguard Station to Rock a Nore   2.90 miles Allow: 1½ hrs

The first Waypost announces that Warren Glen is ¾ mile with the tale of this walk now set – a steepish climb followed by a flat bit and a downhill section, all of varying lengths, until the final descent to Hastings.

The path bends around to the right up the hill towards the unceasing radar dish that commands the shipping in the Channel with a slight whirr.

Continue along the clear path towards and through the kissing gate in front and as the path turns the beauty of this coastline is revealed.

After rain, or in wet weather, the path can itself be challenging never mind the ups and downs.

Down to Warren Glen and follow the signs on the Waypost towards Fairlight Glen ½ mile along The Saxon Shore Way (SSW). You quickly gain height on the short sharp climb, through another annoying kissing gate where I had to take my pack off, and at Post 18 continue the SSW up the steps in front.

There is no disgrace on stopping on the climb as the views looking back are worth the brief respite. The hand rail, first to the right and then to the left provides some modicum of support.

The path flattens out for a few metres before the longish descent into Fairlight Glen. At Post 17 bear left to follow the waymarks for the SSW.

At the bottom of the Glen, bear left up the hill (all the signs have disappeared from the Way Post). Up through the trees, that provide some welcome shade in summer, to more steps and at Post 14, with 2 miles to go to Hastings, bear left up the steps.

The steps up seem interminable.

At Waypost12 bear left to Ecclesbourne Glen and East Hill is 1¼ miles, about 30 minutes walking but at last the path opens out to a view of the sea and that all important bench for a rest after around an hour of walking.

It's the perfect place for a drink and a biscuit before the climb down and up to East Hill and now you can watch the ships go by on the horizon.

The path still rises, Beachey Head appears in front, like an island in a big sea, and below is Rock a Nore but there is a better view from the viewing point in the corner by the bench.

On the opposite side of the glen is the path that winds up through the trees and gorse but first, turn around bear left up the hill for a few metres and then left again down the path that leads to Ecclesbourne Glen that has only just been re-opened after a landslip a few years ago. This heavily wooded valley was once the landing place and entrance for the Iron Age Hill Fort that stood at the centre of East Hill.

Down the steps that sometimes appear to have been built for giants and follow the new steps up the other side, gaining height rapidly to the entrance to East Hill Park and the final climb of the walk.

Keep to the left hand path up to the top of the hill and then down towards the beacon with the Pier in the foreground and the great concrete liner, Marine Court marooned on the seafront in the background. To the right is West Hill where the white terrace shines in the sunlight.

Behind the Beacon are the steps that lead past the entrance to the East Hill lift and the steps down to Rock a Nore but first, take a minute to stand at the viewpoint for some of the best views of Old Town, the broad sweep of Pevensey Bay all the way round to Beachey Head and the ruins of Hastings Castle on West Hill.

Now for the East Hill steps, better going down then climbing up.

Take a minute to stop and stare at the broad sweep of Pevensey Bay all the way round to Beachey Head and closer to the top of the steps are some of the best views of the Old Town, the Pier and the promenade. The ruins of Hastings Castle are on West Hill on the other side of the valley.

Down the steps to the right of the East Hill Lift and at the bottom, turn left towards more steps (Tamarisk Steps) at the end of Tackleway that lead down to Rock-a-Nore.

The Dolphin is at the bottom of the steps, The Royal Standard across the road at the junction with East Parade and The Albion a little further along (the latter two featuring in Book 6: 'Pub Walks in Hastings and St Leonards' and the Dolphin in Book 13: 'More Pub Walks' . There are fish and chip shops galore and even the fun of the fair if weary legs can take such excitement.

If you want to catch the train back to Rye you will need to walk into the centre of Hastings but the bus stop for the Stagecoach 100 and 101 is only a few metres along East Parade opposite the amusements.

The Cove   www.thecovefairlight.co.uk

An utter transformation from the warm brick built former pub into a modern open plan dining pub, reminiscent of a Hastings Net Shop, that offers good dining experience. There's a small area on the right of the bar that could be devoted to drinkers but the saving grace for walkers is the large outdoor garden.

Harvey's Best is on offer and craft ales, a Pig and Porter Skylarking IPA at 4% and a Brewing Brothers Coens at 5% together with a South Downs Cider.

It's still worth the stop though after the ups and downs of this coastal walk although check website to confirm opening hours before your visit.

C Side Café

It's a beautifully formed fit for purpose cafe by the sea with booths, to shelter from the westerly winds, that sit on top of the flood bank to contemplate the views out to sea or inland where Toot Rock is silhouetted against the sky.

It's perfect for that stop at halfway with extremely delicious cakes as well as sausage rolls, paninis and baguettes for the walk ahead to Rye or to Hastings.

Better on good days as it's an outdoor café with no inside seating.

The Dolphin, Rock a Nore   www.thedolphinpub.co.uk

Real Ales

Harveys Best   4%
Hophead   3.8%
Youngs Special 45/

Guest Ales
Proper Job 45/
Bishops Farewell 46/
Chinook   45/

A regular in CAMRA's Good Beer Guide, the 18th century Dolphin was one of the original twelve fisherman's pubs in Hastings Old Town and, although it was rebuilt in 1930, it remains a pub with atmosphere that still preserves the spirit of the original fisherman's pub with photographs that include one of the original, a couple of doors down from the Star in the East.

A pint and seat on the terrace on a good day is a perfect end to the walk looking out over the fisherman's huts and watching the world go by and the cars creating mayhem on Rock a Nore - if you can get a seat.

Dark Star Hophead and Harvey's Best were the nearest to session beers at 3.8 and 4.0 percent and Young's Special brought back memories of London.